ISBN 1 85103 321 1

Originally published as *Claude Debussy Découverte des Musiciens* jointly by Editions Gallimard Jeunesse & Erato Disques.

© & ℗ 2000 by Editions Gallimard Jeunesse & Erato Disques.

This edition first published in the United Kingdom jointly by Moonlight Publishing Ltd, The King's Manor, East Hendred, Oxon OX12 8JY & The Associated Board of the Royal Schools of Music (Publishing) Limited, 24 Portland Place, London W1B 1LU.

English text © & ℗ 2002 by Moonlight Publishing Ltd & The Associated Board of the Royal Schools of Music.

Printed in Italy by Editoriale Lloyd.

Claude
DEBUSSY

FIRST DISCOVERY - MUSIC

Written by Pierre Babin
Illustrated by Charlotte Voake
Narrated by Michael Cantwell

In the summer of 1862, twenty-seven years before the opening of the Eiffel Tower, Claude Debussy was born in Saint-Germain-en-Laye near Paris. He was born with a large bump on his forehead and was baptised Achille-Claude.

A DEBUSSY MUSEUM

The house at 38 rue au Pain still exists. Today it is the Claude Debussy Museum. You can see all sorts of things which belonged to the composer: musical scores, portraits etc... Concerts are often held there. Have you ever been to a museum devoted to music?

When he grew up, he hid the bump under his hair, and chose to use only his second name – Claude. At 38 rue au Pain, where he lives, his parents keep a shop selling china. Unfortunately they are not very good at business.

His parents often move home and Claude's life is not much fun. His father is sent to prison for taking part in the revolution of 1871. In fact, Claude does not know

THE SINGING GLASSES

If you are on your own and bored, try making glasses sing. Take quite a thin glass, wet your finger and rub it around the rim. This will make a continuous sound. If you fill the glass to different levels the sound will change. With three or four glasses you can make a tune!

8

2 STRING QUARTET, OP. 10, 3RD MOVEMENT, ANDANTINO – GENTLY EXPRESSIVE

where his father is. His mother does not look after him very well. He hardly ever goes to school, which he dislikes anyway, because he hates being told what to do! So his mother sends him to Cannes to stay with his godmother, Aunt Octavie, at the Villa 'Rose'.

In Cannes, he sees the sea for the first time in his life and he loves it. One day he goes out on a fishing boat. There is a strong wind and big waves. He is not afraid and when he gets back he says: 'It makes you feel so alive!' Claude wants

WITH A SEASHELL

Hold a shell to your ear: it's as if you can hear the sound of the sea. You can try it with lots of other things: a cup, an empty yoghurt pot, a rolled-up piece of paper... You just need a container through which a little air can pass.

3 LA MER (THE SEA), 'WAVES'

to become a sailor like his father had been when he was younger. He would love to travel and visit faraway countries.

The Villa 'Rose' has a large garden and a piano. Now Claude has plenty to do! He likes to go into the garden and listen to the songs of the birds and the sound of the wind. He wanders into the house and sits at the piano. He tries

4 SONATA FOR FLUTE, VIOLA AND HARP, IST MOVEMENT, PASTORAL

playing a few notes. He listens and listens. He turns listening into a game. The sounds of the notes vibrate in the air like the sounds of the world around him.

TWEET, TWEET

Listen to the birds singing. No-one knows whether they are just talking to each other or singing. What do you think? Are they having a good chat, or simply giving voice for the sheer pleasure of singing?

Aunt Octavie decides he should have piano lessons. His teacher is called Monsieur Cerutti. When he returns to Paris, Claude continues piano lessons with Madame Mauté, who had been taught by the famous pianist Chopin. At the

age of ten he wins a place at the Paris Conservatoire, one of the best music schools in the world. Life gets serious. Now he must learn to play properly and do what his music teachers tell him to do.

GOING ON TO THE NEXT STAGE

Are there things you have taught yourself to do? Maybe playing the trumpet or the xylophone seems easy at first. But watch out! You will reach a point where you can't get any better without the help of a teacher.

At the Conservatoire, Claude is not always a model pupil. At times he amazes his teachers. At other times he disappoints them. Sometimes he shocks them. He wants to be free to write and play just as he likes, and does not

want to do what they tell him. One day, to get his own back for being given a bad mark, he plays a cascade of his favourite chords. It is far too modern for his teacher, who angrily shuts the piano on his fingers!

NOTES THAT GO TOGETHER

Like colours, some notes go together while others do not. Hum a note and hold it and ask a friend to hum a slightly higher note. It will not sound good – you will get the impression that the notes clash or 'rub together'. If your friend then hums higher and higher notes, sooner or later he or she will reach one which sounds really good with yours.

In spite of his rebellious attitude, Claude wins prizes. He gets the chance to work in Russia in a family, where the children call him Bussikov, short for 'De-bussy-kov'. After he returns to Paris, aged twenty-two, he wins the highest award of all, the Prix de Rome. He will go on to write many works for piano, for chorus and for orchestra. Debussy will change the colour of music for ever.

18

THE COLOUR OF MUSIC

Listening to music can make you think of shapes, shades, hazy or clear effects... in other words, pictures. That is normal, because painting and music express the same sorts of things in different ways. What do you 'see' when you listen to the following extract?

Today

as in the past

Debussy's

music

is played

and loved.

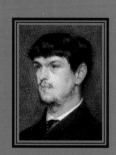

CLAIR DE LUNE

Debussy liked to play the piano whenever he could. He only needed to place his hands on the keyboard and he seemed able to transform the colours and shapes of the world. Many of his compositions were for the piano. It was his favourite way of expressing himself. The way he wrote for the piano was so new that it almost made the piano sound like a different instrument. Some people even said that it was as if the hammers in the piano had disappeared! *Clair de lune* is like taking a walk in a peaceful landscape bathed in moonlight. In *Golliwogg's Cake-Walk* Debussy has translated the jerky, mechanical gestures of a dancing puppet into jazzy music.

Debussy enjoyed the company of his friend the composer Ernest Chausson, and his family.

Debussy grew up as a pianist. He wrote piano music for two hands, four hands and even for two pianos!

20

STRING QUARTET

Debussy wrote very little chamber music (music for a small group of instruments) but the pieces he wrote are all masterpieces. At thirty, he wrote a string quartet. It was one of the first works to make him famous, because the public were astonished by its very distinctive 'colour'. Colour in music is the particular character the composer wants to give to the sound. Like a face, for example, the musical colour can be sad, sunny, sinister, mysterious… In this extract the pizzicato (or plucking of the strings) lends gaiety and energetic colour to the music. Debussy wrote three sonatas at the end of his life, including this one for cello and piano, which is marvellously fresh and dynamic.

22

The Belgian violinist Eugène Ysaÿe (left), with his quartet, was the first to interpret the String Quartet, which Debussy dedicated to him.

The timbre that a musician gives to his instrument when he plays Debussy is special – you can really hear the 'grain' of the sound.

9 STRING QUARTET, OP. 10, 2ND MOVEMENT, RATHER QUICK AND RHYTHMIC
SONATA FOR CELLO AND PIANO, 2ND MOVEMENT, SERENADE

PELLÉAS AND MÉLISANDE

The human voice was our first musical instrument. Singing comes naturally to all of us. Debussy wrote many songs for voice and piano: he wrote tunes to go with the texts of great French poets like Baudelaire or Mallarmé. He also wrote an opera, *Pelléas and Mélisande*. An opera is a story which is sung rather than spoken. *Pelléas and Mélisande* is a love story: Pelléas is in love with Mélisande, a girl with beautiful long hair, but Mélisande is married to the older brother of Pelléas. Debussy enjoyed mystery, secrets and silence. His opera is full of deep and mysterious sounds and silences.

24

In the Tower Scene (above) Pelléas wraps himself in Mélisande's hair as she leans out of the window above him.

The actual story of Pelléas and Mélisande is of uncertain origin, but the opera was first performed in 1902.

THE SEA

Debussy played with the contrasting colours of the instruments in the orchestra in the way a painter uses different coloured paints. His orchestral music is unusual because it leaves the audience with direct impressions or feelings about the sky, the sea… Debussy used to say: 'I love the sea and listen to it with the deep respect which it deserves'. In this passage from the piece called *La Mer* (*The Sea*), listen to the elements fighting with one another: the force of the wind and the singing of the sea. On a quite different note, the *Rhapsody for Clarinet* is full of fantasy and poetry. In *Fêtes* (*Festivals*) you hear a procession mingling with a crowd, and dancing, with flashes of light which illuminate the whole scene!

To illustrate the cover of the score of *La Mer*, Debussy chose the famous Japanese print by Hokusai.

At Houlgate in 1911, Debussy (opposite, on the beach) wrote: 'Here I am with my old friend the sea, which is as immeasurable and beautiful as ever'.

11 LA MER (THE SEA), 'DIALOGUE BETWEEN THE WIND AND THE SEA'
RHAPSODY FOR CLARINET; NOCTURNES, 'FÊTES' ('FESTIVALS')

MOONLIGHT PUBLISHING

Translator:
Penelope Stanley-Baker

ABRSM (PUBLISHING) LTD

Project manager:
Leslie East

Language consultant:
Cathy Ferreira

Text editor:
Lilija Zobens

Editorial supervision:
Caroline Perkins & Rosie Welch

Production:
Simon Mathews & Michelle Lau

English narration recording:
Ken Blair of BMP Recordings

ERATO DISQUES

Artistic and Production Director:
Ysabelle Van Wersch-Cot

KEY: **t** = top **m** = middle **b** = bottom
r = right **l** = left

PHOTOGRAPHIC ACKNOWLEDGEMENTS

© Adagp, Paris 2000 **16**, **19**, **26m**. AKG, Paris **9**, **21**, **23**, **25**. Archives Seuil **26b**. Ph. Cocqueux – Specto **20b**, **24t**. Gershell/Cliché CDM-BGM (Fonds Lefébure) **22t**. Harlingue-Viollet **22m**. Musée C. Debussy, Saint-Germain-en-Laye **6**, **7t**, **15l**. Photo Thierry Martinot **22b**. Photo RMN **12**, **26m**. Photo RMN – G. Blot **19**. Photo RMN – C. Jean **10**. Photo RMN – H. Lewandowski **27**. Roger-Viollet **16**. © Succession H. Matisse **21**.

CD

1. 38 rue au Pain
Prélude à l'après-midi d'un faune
Philippe Jolivet, flute solo
Orchestre Philharmonique de Strasbourg
Conducted by Alain Lombard
℗ Erato Classics, Paris, France 1981

Children's Corner,
'Jimbo's Lullaby'
Monique Haas, piano
℗ Erato Classics, Paris, France 1971

2. Playing truant
String Quartet, Op. 10,
3rd movement, Andantino –
doucement expressif
Keller Quartet
András Keller, János Pilz, violins
Zoltán Gal, viola
Ottó Kertesz, cello
℗ Erato Disques, Paris, France 1994

3. My old friend the sea
La Mer,
'Jeux de vagues'
Orchestre Philharmonique de Strasbourg
Conducted by Alain Lombard
℗ Erato Classics, Paris, France 1981

4. The sound of the wind
Sonata for flute, viola and harp,
1st movement, Pastorale
Jean-Pierre Rampal, flute
Pierre Pasquier, viola
Lily Laskine, harp
℗ Erato Classics, Paris, France 1962

5. Life gets serious
Etudes, Book 1,
'Pour les cinq doigts'
Monique Haas, piano
℗ Erato Classics, Paris, France 1972

6. Dunce or genius?
Etudes, Book 2,
'Pour les accords'
Monique Haas, piano
℗ Erato Classics, Paris, France 1972

7. Leading the way to modern music
Nocturnes,
'Sirènes'
Choeur de l'Opéra du Rhin
Orchestre Philharmonique de Strasbourg
Conducted by Alain Lombard
℗ Erato Classics, Paris, France 1981

8. Piano music
Suite Bergamasque,
'Clair de lune'
Monique Haas, piano
℗ Erato Classics, Paris, France 1972

Children's Corner,
'Golliwogg's Cake-Walk'
Monique Haas, piano
℗ Erato Classics, Paris, France 1972

9. Chamber music
String Quartet, Op. 10,
2nd movement, Assez vif et bien rythmé
Keller Quartet
András Keller, János Pilz, violins
Zoltán Gal, viola
Ottó Kertesz, cello
℗ Erato Disques, Paris, France 1994

Sonata for cello and piano,
2nd movement, Sérénade
Paul Tortelier, cello
Jean Hubeau, piano
℗ Erato Classics, Paris, France, 1962

10. Songs and opera
Pelléas et Mélisande,
The tower scene
Eric Tappy, tenor
Rachel Yakar, soprano
Orchestre National de l'Opéra de
Monte-Carlo
Conducted by Armin Jordan
Editions Durand, Paris
℗ Erato Classics, Paris, France, 1981

11. Orchestral music
La Mer,
'Dialogue du vent et de la mer'
Orchestre Philharmonique de
Strasbourg
Conducted by Alain Lombard
℗ Erato Classics, Paris, France 1981

Rhapsody for clarinet
Antony Morf, clarinet
Orchestre National de l'Opéra de
Monte-Carlo
Conducted by Armin Jordan
℗ Erato Classics, Paris, France, 1981

Nocturnes,
'Fêtes'
Orchestre National de l'Opéra de
Monte-Carlo
Conducted by Armin Jordan
℗ Erato Classics, Paris, France, 1981

JOHANN SEBASTIAN BACH
LUDWIG VAN BEETHOVEN
HECTOR BERLIOZ
FRYDERYK CHOPIN
CLAUDE DEBUSSY
GEORGE FRIDERIC HANDEL
WOLFGANG AMADEUS MOZART
HENRY PURCELL
FRANZ SCHUBERT
ANTONIO VIVALDI